The God and Me! Bible

for Girls ages 2-5

Stories by Su Box

Illustrations by Graham Round

Legacy Press

The God and Me® Bible, Ages 2–5

ISBN 10: 1-58411-088-0
ISBN 13: 978-1-58411-088-0
Legacy reorder#: LP48521

JUVENILE NONFICTION/Religion/Bible Stories

Published in North America by
Legacy Press
P.O. Box 261129
San Diego, CA 92196

First edition 2008

Presented to: _____

From: _____

Date: _____

Contents

Old Testament

New Testament

The Old Testament

God makes the world

At the very beginning of time, there was nothing. The earth was dark and cold and empty. Then God spoke.

"Let there be light!"

Light shone in the darkness and God liked the light.

Then God made the day and the night, huge mountains, rolling hills, and the deep blue sea.

10

God made plants and flowers and trees, stars and planets, the hot sun and the silvery moon.

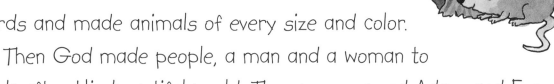

God filled the sea with fish and the air with birds and made animals of every size and color.

Then God made people, a man and a woman to look after His beautiful world. They were named Adam and Eve.

God looked at all He had made. He was pleased with His creation. It was a good world.

Spot the differences

There are eight differences between these two pictures. Put a circle around each of them.

Color by numbers

Use the numbers below to make the butterfly beautiful.

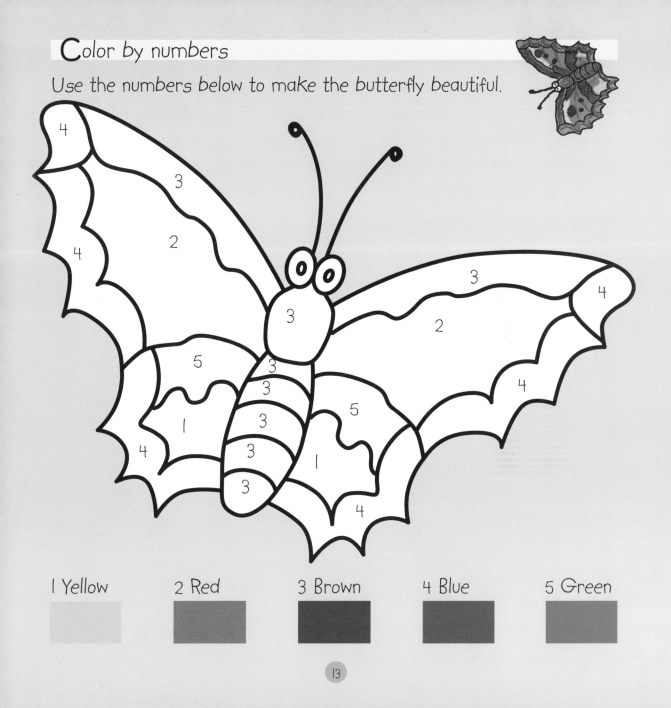

| 1 Yellow | 2 Red | 3 Brown | 4 Blue | 5 Green |

Everything goes wrong

Adam and Eve were very happy.

They chose names for the animals. They ate all the good things that grew in the garden. In the middle of the garden there was a big tree. But God told them they must not eat from that tree.

One day, a snake came and whispered in Eve's ear.

"Look at that yummy fruit," he hissed. "Go on, try it."

Eve looked at the juicy fruit. She reached out and picked some. Then she took a big bite and shared the fruit with Adam who ate it also.

Suddenly they knew that what they did was wrong.

God had given them everything.
But they did the one thing
God told them not to do. They
disobeyed God and everything was spoiled.

Now God could not let them stay in the beautiful garden.

Adam and Eve went away sadly. They could not return.

Find and count

Count how many times
each of these things
appear in the picture of the garden.
Write your answer in the box.

Frog

Rabbit

Blue flower

Crocodile

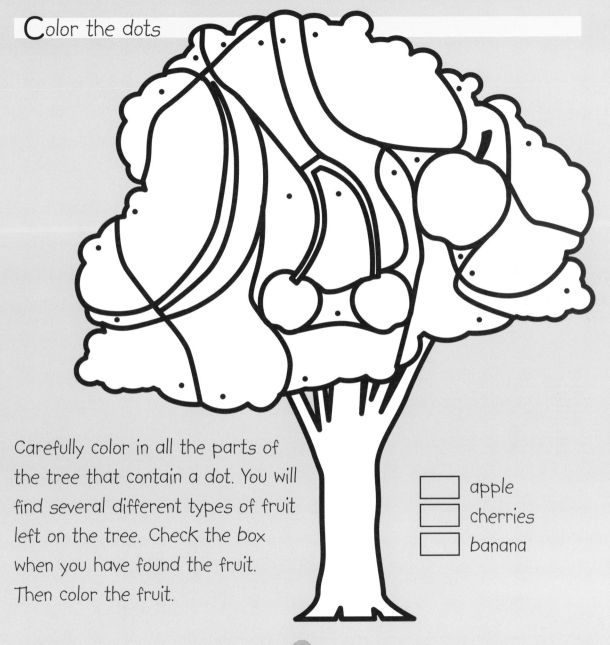

Carefully color in all the parts of
the tree that contain a dot. You will
find several different types of fruit
left on the tree. Check the box
when you have found the fruit.
Then color the fruit.

apple
cherries
banana

17

Noah's ark

God was sad. The beautiful world He made was no longer good. The people He made hurt each other. Noah was the only good man left.

God spoke to Noah. "I will send a flood to wash the world clean. But I will keep you and your family safe. Build an ark, a wooden boat large enough to take your family and two of every kind of animal. Cover it with tar to keep out the water."

Noah obeyed God. He built the ark and collected together all the animals as God told him. Then God shut the door to the ark.

Drop by drop, the rain began to fall. It rained all that day and all the next. Day after day after day, the rain fell down.

Match the pairs

The animals went into the ark in pairs, but some of them have lost their partner. Draw a line connecting the pairs of animals.

Wordsearch

The names of all the animals in the pictures are hidden in the word search below. Put a line through each of them as you find them.

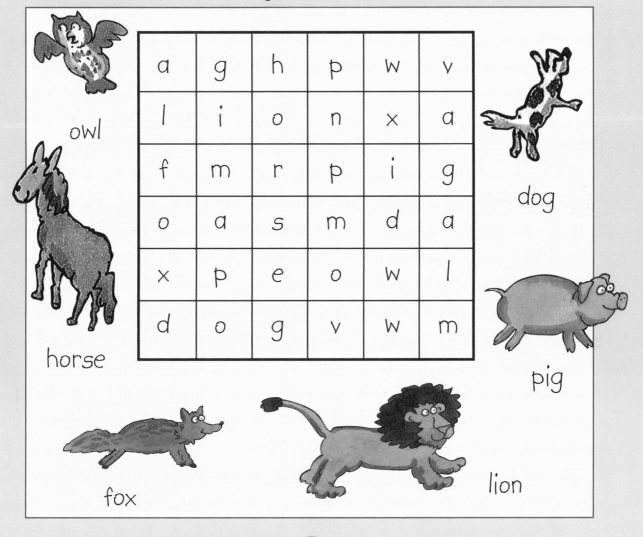

owl

dog

a	g	h	p	w	v
l	i	o	n	x	a
f	m	r	p	i	g
o	a	s	m	d	a
x	p	e	o	w	l
d	o	g	v	w	m

horse

pig

fox

lion

Rain, rain, and more rain

The puddles became streams and the streams became rivers. The rivers became great lakes until there was nothing left to see. Everything was covered by the flood waters.

It rained for forty days and forty nights. Then, one day, everything was still. Everything was quiet. The rain stopped.

God made a strong wind blow until slowly, slowly, the flood waters began to go down.

The ark came to rest on a mountain.

"It is time for you to leave the ark, with your

wife and family and
all the animals, Noah.
Go and make your home
again."

Then the sky was filled with the colors
of a beautiful rainbow.

"The rainbow will remind you of my promise that I will never
again destroy the earth with a flood," God said.

So Noah and all the animals lived on the beautiful land again
and Noah thanked God for keeping them all safe.

Elephant in the maze

Now that all the animals have come out of the ark, can you help the elephants find each other?

Matching parts

Draw a line to connect the correct backs and fronts for each of the different animals.

Abraham's family moves

One day, when Abraham was already quite an old man, God spoke to him.

"I want you to move from here, Abraham, and make your home in a new land. I will look after you and show you where to go. I will make your family into a new nation."

Abraham trusted God. He took his wife Sarah and his nephew, Lot, and all his servants, sheep, and goats and they began their move. They traveled by day and made camp at night, sleeping in tents out under the stars. Abraham went where God told him to go.

When they reached the valley of the River Jordan, Abraham and Lot decided to share the land so that there would be plenty of room for their fluffy sheep and goats to graze on.

Lot went one way and Abraham stayed where he was. Abraham settled in Canaan, the wonderful land God had given to him as his home.

Sheep sizes

Abraham had many fluffy sheep in his flock. Can you put a **B** next to the biggest sheep and an **S** next to the smallest?

How many sheep can you count?

14

Color the picture

Color in the clothes of Abraham and Sarah to complete the picture.

Baby Isaac

Abraham trusted God to keep his
promise to make a nation from Abraham's family. But he and
his wife had no children. Day after day, no baby came.

Then God spoke again to Abraham.

"Look up at the stars, Abraham. Try to count them! You will
have as many descendants as there are stars in the sky."

One day, three men came to visit Abraham.

"Come and rest and have some water to drink," said
Abraham. "Have some food with us." They baked bread and
cooked meat for Abraham's visitors.

Then one of the visitors said,
"We will come back to see you soon.
By then, your wife will be nursing her baby son."

Sarah laughed to herself. She was much too old to have a child.

But sure enough, nine months later, Sarah did have a little baby boy. They called him Isaac, which means "laughter". They were so happy to have their baby!

Star puzzle

How many twinkling stars can you count in this picture of the beautiful night sky? Circle the star that is different.

Dot-to-dot puzzle

Connect all the dots, starting at 1 and ending at 31, to see the wonderful gift God gave to Abraham and Sarah. Use pretty colors to finish the picture.

33

Jacob plays a trick

When Abraham's son Isaac grew up, he married a woman named Rebecca. They had twin sons named Esau and Jacob. Esau was born first. As the oldest son, Esau would receive a special blessing from Isaac.

One day, Esau came home from hunting and found Jacob cooking a delicious meal. "Give me some of that stew!" he asked his brother.

"You can have some stew if you let me have your blessing for being the eldest son," Jacob said quickly.

"You can have anything as long as I can eat now!" said Esau.

Years later, when Isaac was old and almost blind, he asked Esau to go hunting so he could have his favorite meal.

"When you return, I will bless you before I die," Isaac told Esau.

Rebecca was a very smart woman and knew

that she could help Jacob get Isaac's blessing. She cooked for Isaac, and made Jacob wear Esau's clothes so he would smell like Esau. She tied goatskins on to Jacob's arms so he would feel hairy like Esau.

Jacob took the food to his father and Isaac blessed Jacob thinking he was Esau! Even though Jacob was bad and tricked his father, God had special plans for him!

Spot the difference

There are five differences between these two pictures. Circle each one as you find it.

Esau's maze

Esau needs your help! Draw a line to bring Esau back to his tent.

Joseph's beautiful coat

Jacob got married and became the proud father of twelve sons and a daughter. He loved all his children but his favorite was Joseph.

One day, Jacob gave Joseph a beautiful coat to wear. All of his brothers were jealous.

Joseph had strange dreams. He told his brothers about them the next day. But they didn't like what they heard! It sounded as if one day his brothers would bow down and worship Joseph.

The brothers talked among themselves. They became more and more jealous. Why did their father like Joseph the best? They wondered what would happen if Joseph were no longer there.

The brothers wanted to get rid of Joseph. They waited for the right moment...

Color the coat

Use bright colors to make
Joseph's coat beautiful.

40

Counting puzzle

How many fluffy sheep can you count in the picture?

How many of Joseph's brothers do you see?

A slave in Egypt

Joseph's brothers were
out looking after their father's sheep in the fields.

"Here's Joseph, that dreamer!" they said to each other.
"Let's kill him now and throw him into that dry well. We can tell
Dad that a wild animal killed him. He doesn't need to know the
truth."

So the brothers grabbed Joseph, tore his
beautiful coat off him, and threw him into the
well. Joseph was sad.

Then a group of traders passed by on their
way to Egypt.

"Let's sell him to the traders!" said the
jealous brothers.

So Joseph was sold as a
slave and taken to Egypt. He was afraid and sad he would
never see his dad again. The brothers dipped his coat in
goat's blood and told his father that Joseph was dead.

But God had wonderful plans for Joseph. Years later, his
dreams came true. When his brothers went to Egypt looking
for food, they bowed down to the new ruler, second only to the
king. They were surprised that it was their brother Joseph!
Joseph invited his father, his brothers, and all of their families
to live with him in Egypt.

Colored bundles

This camel is carrying many
heavy bundles.
How many of each color
is she carrying?

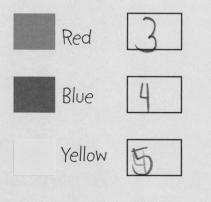

Red   3

Blue   4

Yellow 5

There are six birds hidden in the picture above.
Circle the ones you can find.

45

The baby in the basket

Many years after Joseph's family moved to Egypt, the new King began to fear the number of God's people who lived in Egypt. First he made them his slaves. Then he told his soldiers to drown the baby sons of each Israelite family in the Nile River!

But one brave mother hid her baby to protect him. When the baby was too big to hide, she made a basket and put her baby in it. Then she hid the basket among the reeds on the Nile River.

Miriam, the baby's big sister, watched over the baby and saw the king's daughter come down to the river to bathe. Then the baby cried out.

"A baby!" said the princess, picking him up. The princess was so happy to find him.

"I know someone who can feed the baby," said Miriam, and she ran to fetch her own mother.

"Look after the baby for me until he is big enough to live in the palace," said the princess, "and I will pay you." The brave mother and her baby Moses were together again!

Help the stork!

The stork is trying to catch fish for dinner. Draw over the lines which go from his big beak to the slippery fish.

Connect the pairs

There are two of each of these animals in the picture.
Draw a line between the pairs.

frog

fish

stork

duck

beetle

Let my people go

God sent Moses to rescue his people from the cruel new King of Egypt.

"God wants you to let his people go," said Moses.

"I don't know this God," the King said. "I will not let my slaves go."

"Then terrible things will happen in Egypt!" said Moses.

First, God made the water in the Nile River turn to blood. But the King would not let God's people go. Then the land was covered in frogs and biting insects. All the working animals became ill and died. Bad sores appeared on the skin of all the Egyptians.

Hailstones pelted the land and locusts ate all the crops. Then
the land went dark. There was no sun shining in the Egyptian
sky. But, no matter what, the King would not let God's people go.
Finally, the firstborn son of every Egyptian family died.
The King of Egypt lost his son, too. He sent for Moses.
"Take your people," he shouted. "I will let them go."

How many frogs?

Add up the number of bouncy frogs in each row and write the answer in the box.

Odd one out

Three of these pictures of Moses are the same, but one is different.

Write the number of the one that is different here.

The great escape

Moses led God's people out of Egypt toward the Red Sea. God was with them, day and night.

But as soon as the slaves left, the King of Egypt became angry and changed his mind.

"What will I do without my slaves?" he wailed. "Get my war chariot ready. We must bring them back!"

When they saw the King coming, God's people knew they were trapped. The Red Sea was in front of them; the Egyptian army was behind them.

"Don't be afraid!" Moses told them. "God will keep you safe!"

Moses held his staff out over the deep waters of the Red Sea and the people watched as a clear path opened up for them so they could cross on dry land. Once God's people had crossed, Moses held out his staff again. A mighty wind blew back the water to cover the path and the Egyptian army who were following. God's people were safe and praised Him on their way to the land God had promised them.

Silly sheep

Can you see what is wrong with each of these pictures? Put a circle around the mistake.

Complete the picture

Can you find where these shapes fit in the main picture? Write the number of the space next to the piece.

a

b

c

d

e

Joshua and the battle of Jericho

God chose Joshua to be the next leader of his people.

"Don't be afraid, Joshua," said God. "I will be with you wherever you go."

On their way to the promised land, the Israelites had to pass through the city of

Jericho. The city had tall walls and strong city gates and lots of guards. They would not let the Israelites in.

God told Joshua what to do: "Tell seven priests to march around Jericho once every day for six days. On the seventh day they must march around the city seven times while the priests blow their special trumpets. And at the last trumpet blast, everyone must shout as loudly as they can."

Everyone obeyed God – and the walls of the city fell down with a CRASH!

How many priests?

Write the number of priests you see in the box.

How many have yellow belts?

How many have blue belts?

Jerico maze

Help the priest find his way into Jericho.

Samuel's sleepless nights

"Please, God, give me a baby," Hannah prayed again and again. God heard her prayers and baby Samuel was born.

When Samuel was old enough, Hannah took him to stay with Eli the priest. Samuel would help the old man serve God.

One night, when Samuel was in bed, he heard a voice call, "Samuel! Samuel!"

"Here I am," said Samuel, running to Eli.

"I did not call you" said Eli. "Go back to bed." So Samuel went back to bed.

It happened again. And Eli sent Samuel back to bed. And again...

This time, Eli said, "God is calling you, Samuel. Next time

say, 'Speak, Lord,
your servant is listening!'"

So Samuel went back to bed.

"Samuel! Samuel!" came the voice. Samuel did what Eli told him.

"Speak, Lord, your servant is listening!" said Samuel.

God told Samuel many things about the people of Israel. Everything God said came true.

Spot the differences

Find eight differences between the two pictures and draw a circle around each of them.

Dot-to-dot

Connect the dots to find something which helped Samuel see at night.

The shepherd boy

A farmer named Jesse had eight sons. The youngest, David, was a shepherd. He took care of his father's sheep and kept them safe from wild animals.

One day the prophet Samuel visited Jesse. God told him He had chosen one of Jesse's sons to be the next King.

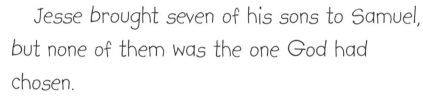

Jesse brought seven of his sons to Samuel, but none of them was the one God had chosen.

"Do you have any more sons?" asked Samuel.

"Yes," said Jesse. "Young David is looking after the sheep. I'll send for him."

When Samuel saw David, he heard God's voice saying, "He is the one I want to be King."

So Samuel poured oil on David's head to show that God had chosen him. From that day, David knew God was always with him.

Match the pair

Only two of these pictures of David are exactly the same.
Circle the two that match.

1 2 3 4

5 6 7 8

Complete the picture

Color in the hats and headdresses in the picture below.

David and the giant

David's brothers were soldiers in King Saul's army and had gone to fight the Philistines. One day, David went to visit them.

Suddenly he heard a man shouting loudly. It was Goliath the giant, the Philistine's biggest and strongest soldier. Everyone in King Saul's army was afraid of Goliath.

"I'm not afraid of this man!" said David. "I will fight him!"

Carrying his sling, David picked up five stones from a stream. He walked toward Goliath.

The giant gave a nasty laugh when he saw little David. "You have a sword and a spear," said David, "but God is on my side!"

David put a stone in his sling, spun it around his head, and let go. The stone hit Goliath's forehead and he fell to the ground with a THUD!

The terrified Philistines ran away as fast as they could! God had given David the victory.

70

Find the words

Can you find these words hidden in the grid?
Draw a circle around each word.

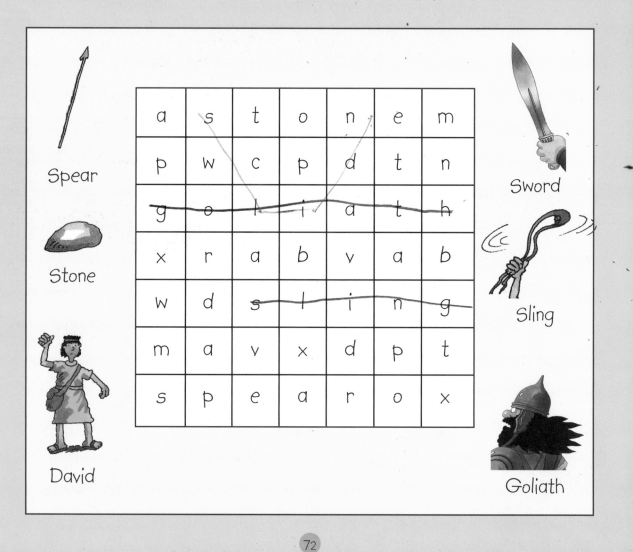

a	s	t	o	n	e	m
p	w	c	p	d	t	n
g	o	l	i	a	t	h
x	r	a	b	v	a	b
w	d	s	l	i	n	g
m	a	v	x	d	p	t
s	p	e	a	r	o	x

Spear

Stone

David

Sword

Sling

Goliath

Count the spears

How many of the soldiers in the picture are carrying spears?

How many of the soldiers have no spear?

How many soldiers are there in the picture?

God looks after Elijah

One day God sent the prophet Elijah to speak with King Ahab. Ahab was a bad King who worshipped the false god of Baal.

"Change your ways. Be a good King or God won't let it rain," Elijah warned the King.

Ahab would not change. God stopped the rain just as He said. The country was dry. There was no water.

But God looked after Elijah and sent ravens to carry food to him. God also made sure Elijah had enough water to drink.

Some time later, God sent Elijah to a Kind woman.

She had very
little left to eat and
there was still no rain. The
nice lady shared her last loaf of bread
with Elijah. But now she had no more food for
her and her family.

"Don't worry," said Elijah. "God says your flour and oil will
never run out until the day it rains again!"

Sure enough, there was always enough to feed them,
just as God promised.

Big and small

Put a **B** next to the biggest raven and an **S** by the smallest.

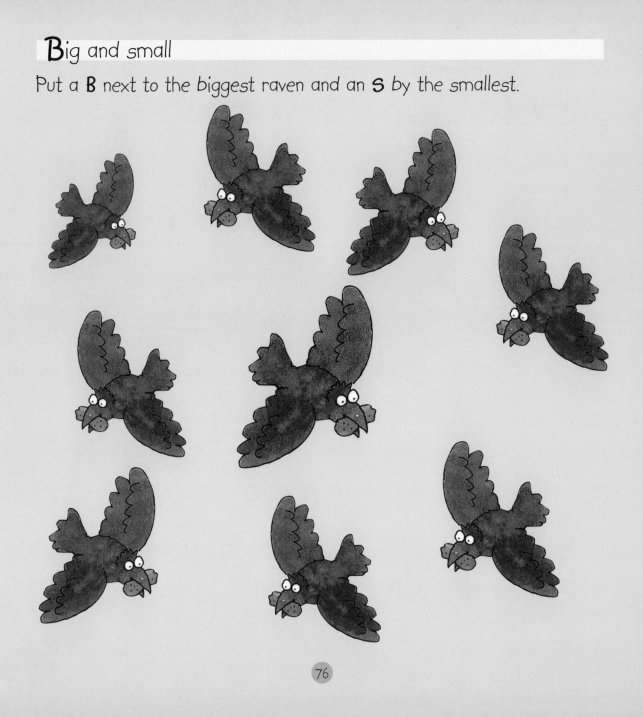

Find these objects in the big picture and draw a circle round them.

Trees

Plate

Bread

Cup

Bowl

Elijah

Fire from heaven

It had not rained for three years. God sent Elijah back to King Ahab.

"God is going to show you who that He is the one true God," Elijah said to the King.

"We will have a competition. Tell the prophets of Baal to come to Mount Carmel. They will put a bull on their altar. I will put another bull on the altar of the Lord. We will call on the one true God to send fire – and see who answers!"

The prophets of Baal shouted all day, but no fire came.

"Shout louder!" said Elijah. "Baal isn't listening! Or maybe he's asleep!"

Still Baal did not answer.

Then Elijah asked his servants to pour water on the altar. Soon water covered the entire altar.

"Please God, show these people that You are the true God of Israel!" Elijah prayed loudly.

Whoosh! Fire flashed down from heaven and burned up everything on Elijah's altar even though it was soaking wet!

Everyone was amazed and shouted, "The Lord is God!"

Match the picture

Only one of these prophets is exactly like the one in the box.
Put a check next to him.

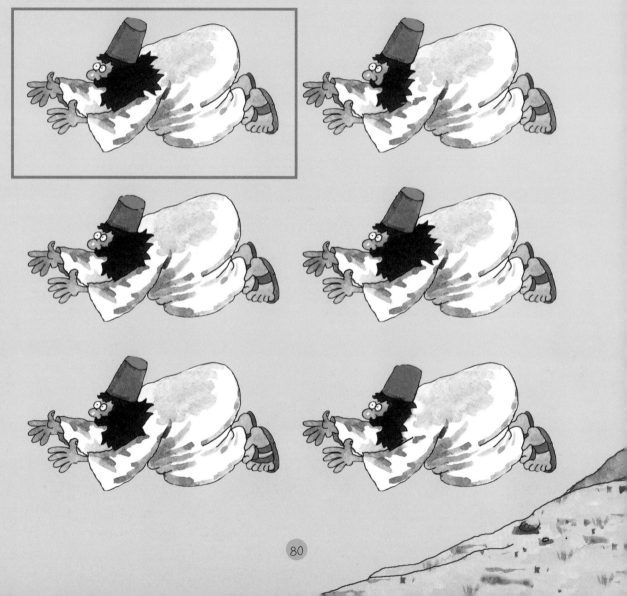

Beautiful Colors

Trace the word for each answer.

Elijah's robe is: red

Elijah's headdress is: green

The prophets' hats are: blue

The flames are: red and yellow

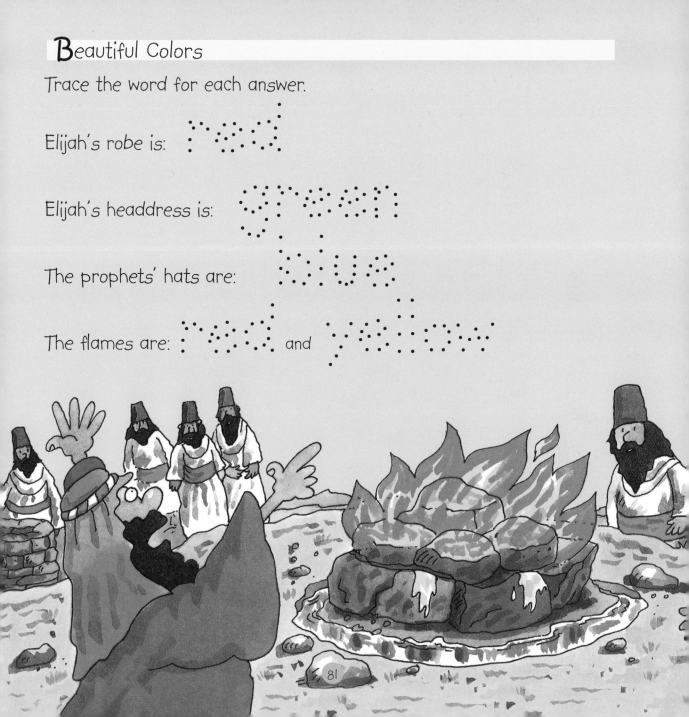

The little servant girl

There was a little girl who was taken from Israel to be a servant in Syria. She worked for Naaman, a brave soldier in the Syrian army.

One day Naaman became sick. His skin turned white and sore and no one could help.

The little girl said, "Go and see God's prophet Elisha! He can make you better!"

So Naaman went to see Elisha.

Elisha said, "Go and wash seven times in the Jordan River."

Naaman was angry. "The rivers in Syria are just as good as this river!"

"Just try it and see," said Naaman's servants.

So Naaman went down to the river. He dipped himself in it seven times. Immediately, his skin was soft and healthy again!

Naaman went back to Elisha and said, "Now I know that there is no god but the God of Israel."

Find the ducks

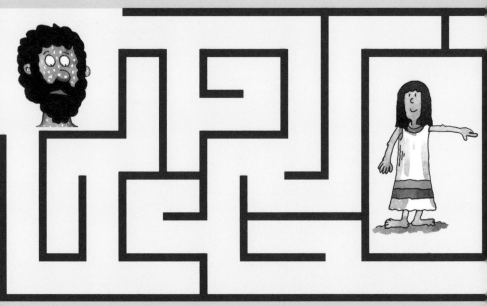

How many ducks can you see in the picture?
Draw a circle around each of them. Write the
number in the box.

Naaman's Maze

Help Naaman
find his way
to the Jordan
River.

Daniel in the lions' den

Daniel, a faithful servant of God, was taken as a prisoner to a far-away country. But Daniel still trusted God and prayed to Him each day.

The king liked Daniel and gave him an important job. Daniel worked hard and did a good job. Daniel's success made people jealous.

"Make a law," his enemies said to the king. "People must pray only to you or they will be thrown to the lions."

The King liked this idea so he made the law.

But Daniel still prayed to God. His enemies told the king, so Daniel had to be thrown to the hungry lions.

The King worried about Daniel all night.

In the morning the King ran to the lions' den.

"Daniel!" he shouted.

"The lions didn't hurt me!" Daniel called. "God sent an angel to shut their mouths."

The King was very happy. He set Daniel free, and he sent his enemies into the lions' den instead!

Color the dots

Color in all the shapes marked with a dot to find out what is hiding in the cave.

Write down the answer in the box.

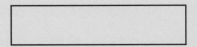

Count the lions

How many times can you find the word 'lion' in the grid below? ☐

x	l	a	w	v	l
l	i	o	n	a	i
m	o	p	l	w	o
r	n	l	i	o	n
v	p	s	o	t	a
l	i	o	n	x	w

Jonah runs away

God spoke to Jonah: "Go to Nineveh! Tell everyone there that I know all the bad things they are doing!"

But Jonah did not do as God asked. He was afraid. He ran away and got on a ship sailing far away.

Jonah settled down to sleep as the ship sailed away.

While Jonah was sleeping, God sent a big storm. The wind blew stronger and stronger. The waves splashed higher and higher.

All the sailors were very scared.

"Wake up!" they said to Jonah. "We're going to sink!"

Jonah shouted, "It's my fault! I ran from God. You must throw me overboard!"

So the sailors threw him into the sea. The storm stopped – the sailors were safe again.

Jonah was sinking deep into the sea when

God sent a huge fish to swallow him up!

While inside the fish, Jonah prayed to God. "I'm sorry that I didn't obey you."

Three days later, the fish spat Jonah out onto the beach.

"Go to Nineveh," God said again.

This time Jonah obeyed. The people of Nineveh listened to him and turned back to God.

Jonah's ship trip

Color in this picture of Jonah being thrown into the sea.

Find the fish

How many huge fish can you find in the sea?

Solutions to the puzzles from the Old Testament

God makes the world Pages 12 - 13

• The differences are circled on the picture.

Everything goes wrong Pages 16 - 17

• 1 frog; 2 rabbits; 3 blue flowers; 1 crocodile

Noah's ark Pages 20 - 21

• The words are circled in the word search.

a	g	h	p	w	v
l	i	o	n	x	a
f	m	r	p	i	g
o	a	s	m	d	a
x	p	e	o	w	l
d	o	g	v	w	m

Rain, rain, and more rain Pages 24 - 25

Abraham's family moves Pages 28 - 29

S

B

• There are 13 sheep.

Baby Isaac Pages 32 - 33

• There are 12 stars.

• The odd one out is circled on the picture.

Jacob plays a trick Pages 36 - 37

•The answers are circled on the picture.

Joseph's beautiful coat Pages 40 - 41

• There are 8 sheep in the picture.

• There are 10 brothers in the picture.

A slave in Egypt Pages 44 - 45

• The answers are circled on the picture.

• 3 red bundles., 4 blue bundles, 5 yellow bundles.

The baby in the basket Pages 48 - 49

Let my people go Pages 52 - 53

• 2 frogs, 4 frogs, 3 frogs, 5 frogs, and 6 frogs.

• Picture 2 is the odd one out.

The great escape Pages 56 - 57

• The answers are circled on the pictures

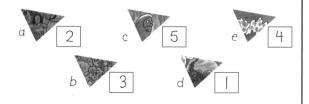

a 2   c 5   e 4

b 3   d 1

Joshua and the battle of Jericho Pages 60 - 61

• The are 7 priests.
3 are wearing
yellow belts.
4 are wearing
blue belts.

Samuel's sleepless night Pages 64 - 65

• The answers are circled on the picture.

The shepherd boy Pages 68 - 69

Drawings 2 and 8 are the same.

David and the giant Pages 72 - 73

• The answers are circled in the grid.

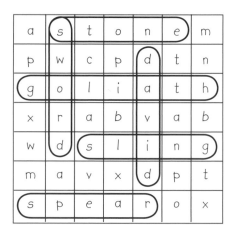

a	s	t	o	n	e	m
p	w	c	p	d	t	n
g	o	l	i	a	t	h
x	r	a	b	v	a	b
w	d	s	l	i	n	g
m	a	v	x	d	p	t
s	p	e	a	r	o	x

• 6 soldiers are carrying spears.
4 soldiers have no spears.
There are 10 soldiers in the picture.

God looks after Elijah Pages 76 - 77

S

B

• The answers are circled on the picture.

Fire from heaven Pages 80 - 81

The little servant girl
Pages 84 - 85

• There are 5 ducks in the picture.

Daniel in the lion's den Pages 88 - 89

• A lion is hiding in the cave.

• The word 'lion' appears 6 times in the grid; they are circled below.

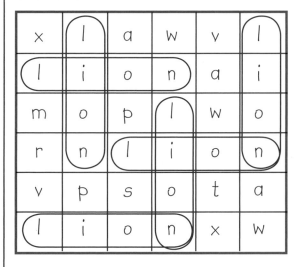

Jonah runs away Pages 92 - 93

• There are 6 hugh fish in the sea.

98

The New Testament

Mary's baby

Mary and Joseph lived in Nazareth. Soon they were going to be married.

One day Mary had a big surprise – one of God's angels visited her.

"Mary, don't be afraid," said the angel. "God has chosen you to have a baby boy. You will name Him Jesus.

He is God's Son – the savior God has promised."

Mary was a little scared. But she wanted to obey God.

"I will do what God wants," she said. Mary trusted God.

One day, Joseph told Mary they were taking a trip.

"We must go to Bethlehem, my family's hometown. The Roman ruler wants to count everyone."

Mary and Joseph arrived in Bethlehem after a long journey. But there was nowhere to stay in the busy little town. When Mary's baby was born she made a bed for him in a manger.

How many little mice can you find in the picture?

Complete the pictures

All these creatures have something missing.

Draw in the owl's beak.

Draw the big ears on the donkey.

Draw the sharp horns on the ox.

The angel and the shepherds

On the hills near Bethlehem, shepherds
were looking after their sheep. Suddenly, the
sky was filled with a blinding light and they saw an angel!

"Don't be afraid!" said the angel. "I have good news for you!
Tonight in Bethlehem God's promised King has
been born! You will find the baby lying in a
manger."

Then the sky was filled with more angels,
praising God. It was a wonderful sight!

The shepherds left their sheep at once

and hurried off to Bethlehem.

"We must go to see this special baby!" they said.

There they found Mary and Joseph and the baby lying in the manger. "It's all just as the angel said!" they exclaimed.

The shepherds went back to their sheep, praising God for the wonderful things they had seen.

Wordsearch

Draw a circle around the words the angel said to the shepherds.

afraid   good   news   baby   king   manger

m	o	d	b	k	p
a	f	r	a	i	d
n	s	k	b	n	s
g	r	t	y	g	s
e	g	o	o	d	a
r	a	n	e	w	s

106

Join the dots

Join the dots to see what the shepherd is carrying.

How many sheep can you count on this page?

The wise men worship Jesus

Far from Bethlehem some wise men were studying the stars. They spotted a new star, shining brightly in the sky.

"It means a new king has been born!" they said. "We must travel to find him. We will take gifts to honor him!"

So the wise men packed their bags and set off, always following the star.

After a very long journey, the wise men reached Bethlehem.

"Look! The star is shining over that house!" they said excitedly.

They went quietly into the house and found Mary, Joseph, and Jesus.

The wise men knelt down before the child and worshipped Him.

"We have found the new king!" they said.

Then they gave Jesus precious gifts: gold, frankincense, and myrrh.

The wise men were so happy!

Missing gifts

The wise men have their gifts hidden on their clothes. Draw a circle around the gifts and color them in.

Wise man maze

Show the wise man the correct way to reach the star over the house where he will find Jesus.

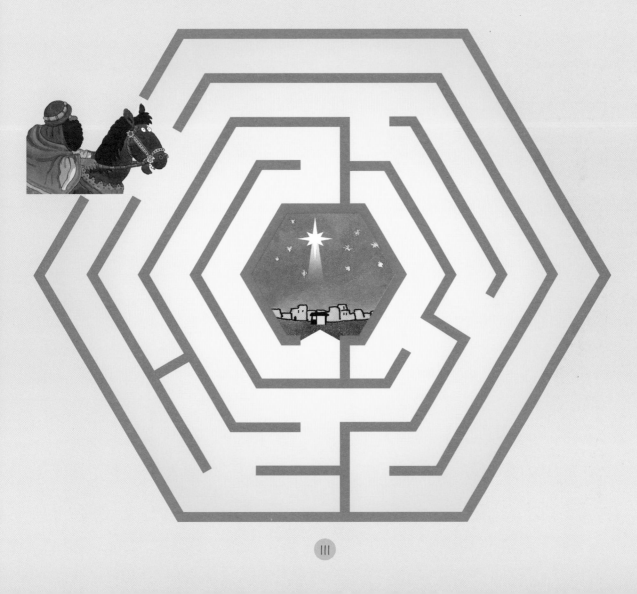

The four fishermen

Jesus grew and began to talk to people about God. Crowds of people came to listen.

One day, Jesus asked two fishermen for help. He wanted everyone to see and hear Him. So the fishermen – Simon and Andrew – let Jesus stand in their boat.

When Jesus finished speaking, he told Simon to push the boat out and let down the fishing nets.

"We were fishing all night but didn't catch anything," said Simon. But he did what Jesus said. Suddenly, the nets were full of slippery, shiny fish!

The nets were very heavy, so James and John
– Simon's friends – came out to help pull up the
nets.

Simon was amazed. It was a miracle!

"Don't be afraid," said Jesus. "Follow me!"

The four fishermen were Jesus'
first disciples, His special
friends.

Complete the picture

Each of these shapes belong in the big picture. Write the number of the space next to the shape where it belongs.

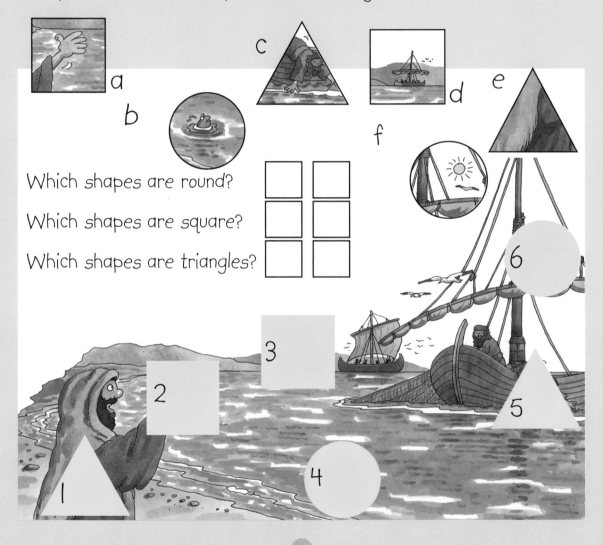

a

b

c

d

e

f

Which shapes are round?

Which shapes are square?

Which shapes are triangles?

Count the colors

Count the number of fish of each color in the net.

How many red fish? ☐   How many blue fish? ☐

How many yellow fish? ☐   How many fish altogether? ☐

115

Jesus meets Matthew

Matthew was a tax collector. He
did not have many friends because tax collectors
often stole extra money and kept it for themselves.

One day, Matthew had a visitor. It was Jesus.

"Follow me!" said Jesus.

At once, Matthew got up, left everything and
became one of Jesus' special friends.

Matthew asked Jesus to a great feast in his house.
There was wonderful food for everyone. It was
a huge celebration.

116

"Why do you hang out with bad people like tax collectors?" a man asked Jesus.

"I've come to help all people who need me," He answered.

Matthew had spent his life counting money and taxes. Now he left his money behind and started following Jesus.

Find the mistakes

Can you find six things which don't belong in this picture?

Mark them with an "X."

How much?

Tax collectors counted money.
Add up the coins to get the sums.

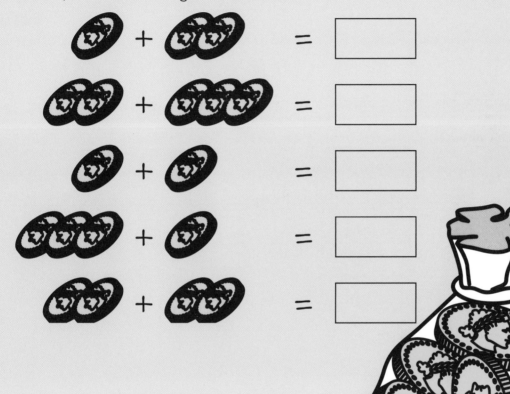

How many coins are
there in the bag?

The four good friends

There was a man who couldn't walk. His four friends carried him to see Jesus. He could make the man well.

When they got to the house where Jesus was staying, they could not get in! There were too many people inside. Then one friend had an idea.

"Let's go up to the roof," he said.

The men carried their friend up the outside steps and pushed away the mud and branches on the roof until there was a big hole.

Then the men carefully lowered the man down into the crowd in front of Jesus.

"Pick up your mat," said Jesus. "You can walk home by yourself now."

The four friends smiled. Everyone was so surprised! The man got up and went home. Jesus had made him well.

Which rope?

Only one of these ropes is still connected to the stretcher.

Which one is it? ☐

Spot the difference

Can you circle the seven differences between these two pictures?

A strong foundation

Jesus told many stories to the crowds who followed Him. One day He told this story:

"If you listen to my words and obey them, you will be like a wise man who built his house upon a rock.

"Two men were building houses. The first man took a long time to build his house because he built a strong stone house on a solid rock foundation. He was wise."

124

"The second man was lazy. He quickly built a house on loose sand. He was foolish.

"One day the weather turned bad! The rain poured down, strong winds blew and the rivers flooded.

"The house on the rock stood firm and did not fall. The wise man was happy that he had worked hard to build a strong house.

"The foolish man saw cracks in his walls. The cracks grew bigger and bigger ... then the house on the sand fell down with a CRASH!

"Be like the wise man," said Jesus. "Listen to my words and do what I say, and you will be safe."

Maze

Help the wise man and the foolish man find the way to their own houses.

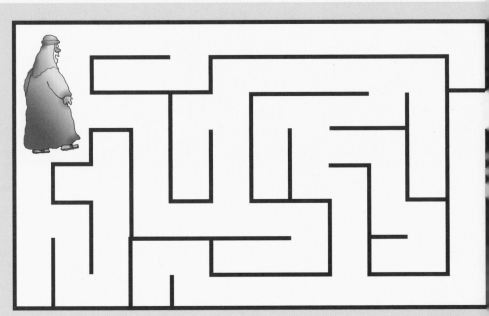

Opposites

Draw a line to match those words which have opposite meanings in the story.

rock   fell down

long time   foolish

wise   sand

stood firm   quickly

The big storm

"Let's sail to the other side of the lake," said Jesus to His friends one day.

Jesus was tired and soon fell asleep in the boat.

Suddenly a huge storm started. The little boat was tossed around and began to fill with water!

Jesus didn't notice the storm. He was still sound asleep.

"Wake up! Wake up!" the frightened disciples called to Jesus. "We're going to sink!"

Jesus woke up. Then He stood up and said, "Wind, be quiet. Waves, calm down."

At once the storm vanished.

"Look, even the winds and waves obey Him!" said the disciples in amazement.

Who's there?

Which of these people sailed in the boat? Put a check next to them.

Word search

Find the words about storms in the grid. Which word means the opposite of a storm? Circle it on the grid in red.

storm   wind   calm   rain   wave   water

s	t	o	r	m	v
m	o	c	a	l	m
r	s	w	i	n	d
a	w	a	v	e	s
i	w	a	t	e	r
n	c	k	a	m	s

The girl who Jesus healed

One day, a crowd gathered to see Jesus. A man named Jairus called out to Him: "Jesus! Please help me! My only daughter is dying!"

On the way to Jairus' house they met one of his servants.

"It's too late," said the servant. "The girl is dead." Jairus was broken hearted.

But Jesus said, "Don't be afraid. Trust Me and she will be well."

Everyone at Jairus' house was crying – they were very sad because they loved the little girl.

"Don't worry," said Jesus kindly, "she is not dead. She is just sleeping." Everyone was confused.

Jesus took the girl's hand and gently said, "Get up, my child."

She sat up – she was alive! It was a miracle.

Her parents were very happy and they thanked Jesus with all their hearts.

Left or right?

Write 'r' in the box next to the right hands and 'l' in the box next to the left hands.

Top and bottom

Draw a line to match the heads to the bodies of the people from the story picture.

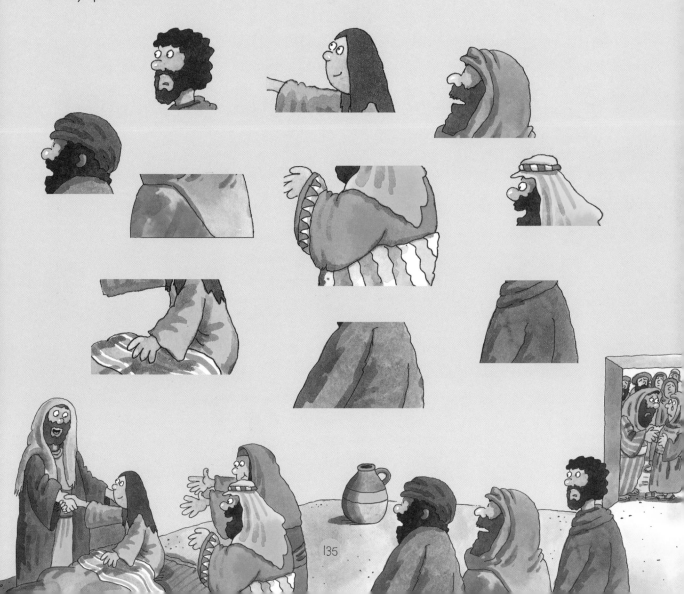

135

The big picnic

A huge crowd of people had been listening to Jesus all day. The sun was beginning to go down and everyone was hungry.

"Give them something to eat," Jesus said to His disciples.

"There's a young boy here who gave us five loaves and two fish," said Andrew. "That will never be enough for all of these people."

Jesus took the loaves and fish, gave thanks to God, and broke the food into pieces.

His friends shared the food with all of the people in the huge crowd. It was like a big picnic.

To everyone's surprise there was plenty for the whole crowd. No one went hungry!

Later the disciples gathered up enough leftovers to fill twelve baskets.

Jesus had taken what little the boy offered and used it to bless many other people.

Large, small, and different

Put a check next to the biggest loaf and the biggest fish.

Put an "X" next to the smallest loaf and the smallest fish.

How many loaves are in this puzzle?

How many fish can you see here?

Which fish is different?

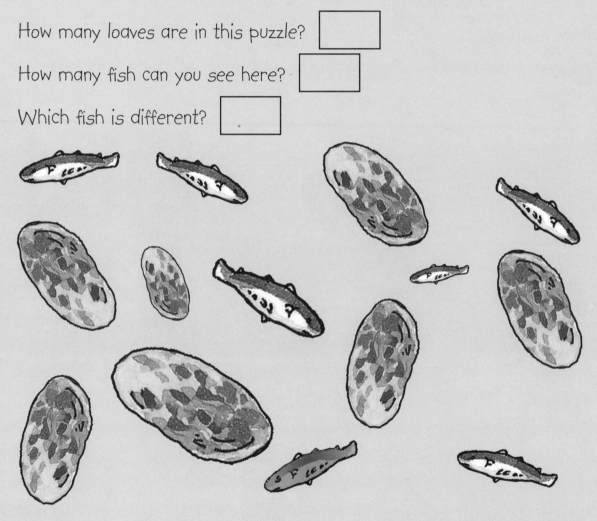

The good neighbor

Jesus told this story about how to be kind to other people:

"A man was walking down the road from Jerusalem to Jericho all by himself. Suddenly robbers jumped out from behind a rock. They took his money and his clothes and hurt him very badly. The poor man couldn't move.

"Then he heard footsteps – someone would finally help him. But the other man walked on by without stopping to help.

"Later he heard more footsteps.

"He will help me!" thought the man.

"But this second man walked past him too.

"Then a Samaritan came along the road. He rushed over to help the injured man even though Samaritans were not known for being helpful people.

"He bandaged the man's cuts and gave
him a drink of water. Then he put the man on his
donkey and took him to an inn. He paid the innkeeper to take
care of the man."

Then Jesus said to the people listening to the story, "Go
and be like that kind man too."

Spot the difference

These four donkeys all have one detail which is different from the other three. Put a circle around each difference.

Trace the word

Donkey

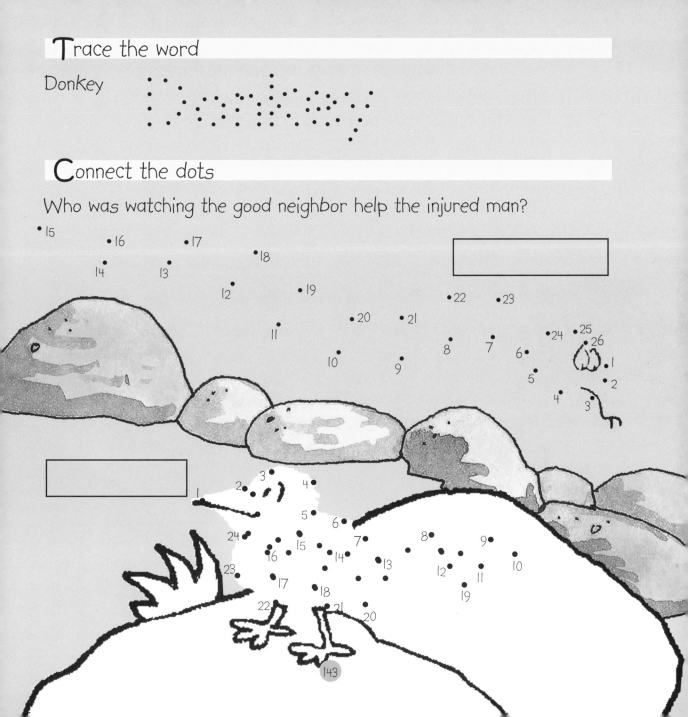

Connect the dots

Who was watching the good neighbor help the injured man?

143

The lost sheep

Jesus told this story about a kind and loving shepherd:

"A shepherd once had a hundred sheep. He knew them all, looked after them well, and kept them safe from wild animals.

"One day, the shepherd found that one sheep was missing! Where could it be? He wanted to find him.

"He made sure the other ninety-nine were safe and then started to look for the lost sheep.

"He looked everywhere: beneath bushes, beside the stream and behind rocks. Suddenly he heard a faint 'baa-aa'.

"He rushed toward the sound. Yes, he had found his lost sheep!

"The shepherd put the lost sheep on his shoulders and carried it carefully home.

"He was so pleased to find his sheep that he held a special celebration with his friends.

"God is like that shepherd," said Jesus. "He cares even if just one of his sheep is lost."

Count the sheep

How many *sheep* can you count in this picture?

How many *sheeps'* ears can you see?

How many *sheeps'* legs can you see?

146

Shepherd's maze

Help the shepherd return to the rest of the flock.

Jesus heals the blind man

A poor blind man sat
begging at the roadside every day.

One day, he heard a crowd of excited people
saying: "Jesus!" "Let's see Jesus!" "Jesus can heal people!"

"That's what I want," thought the man.

He stood up and shouted out: "Jesus! Have mercy on me!"

Other people in the crowd told him to be quiet..

But Jesus stopped and asked kindly, "What do
you want me to do for you?"

"I want to be able to see!" he said.

"Then see!" said Jesus. "Your faith in me has made you well!'

At once, the man's eyes became clear and he could see.

"Thanks be to God!" shouted the man. "I can see! I can see!"

Find and count

One of the people below is not in the crowd above.

Write his or her letter in the box. ☐

How many children can you see in the crowd? ☐

How many grown-ups can you see in the crowd? ☐

a   b   c   d

Find the differences

Can you spot eight differences between these two pictures?
Draw a circle around them when you find them.

The little tax collector

Zacchaeus was a tax collector in Jericho. No one liked him. He cheated and stole people's money.

One day, Zacchaeus heard that Jesus was coming to Jericho. He wanted to see Jesus.

Zacchaeus was very short. He couldn't see over the crowds of people waiting for Jesus.

"I'll climb a tree!" thought Zacchaeus. He climbed into the branches and waited.

Jesus came closer. Suddenly He stopped – right beneath the tree!

"Zacchaeus, hurry down!" said Jesus, "I must come to your house today."

Zacchaeus could hardly believe it. He didn't have any friends. Why would Jesus want to speak to him?

He climbed down and welcomed Jesus into his house.

Jesus and Zacchaeus talked for a long time.

Afterwards he told Jesus, "I will give away half of all I own and repay everyone I have cheated."

Meeting Jesus had changed Zacchaeus forever.

Where is he?

Zacchaeus is hidden in the trees. Draw a circle to show where he is.

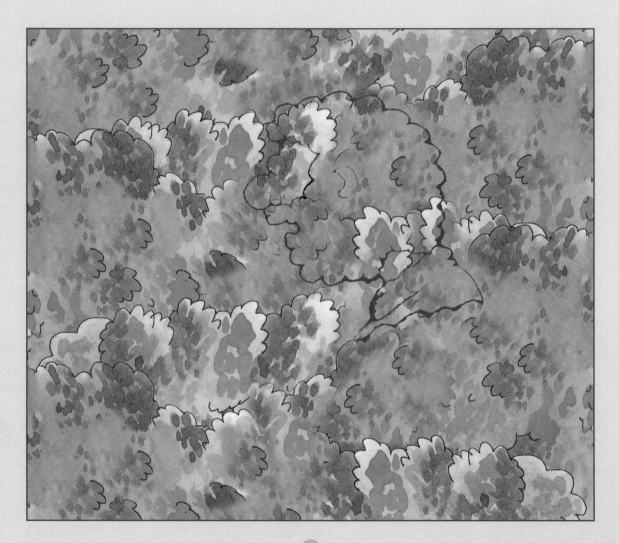

Odd one out

Which of these people is different from all the others? Draw a circle around him.

Colors

The people are wearing colorful clothes. Draw a line to connect the people with their descriptions:

a lady with a yellow robe

a man with a blue belt

a man with a green headdress

a man in a brown coat

The king rides on a donkey

It was time for a special Hebrew festival called Passover. Jesus and lots of other people were going to Jerusalem to celebrate.

Jesus said to two friends, "You will find a young donkey in the village. Untie it and bring it to Me. You can tell the owner that your master needs it."

The disciples did what Jesus said.

Then Jesus got on the donkey and rode into Jerusalem.
Great crowds of people cheered for Jesus. They waved palm
branches high in the air and spread their coats on the road to
honor Him.

"Hosanna!" they shouted. "God bless the promised King!
Glory to God!"

Jesus was joyfully welcomed into the city.

Path to Jerusalem

Draw a path to show Jesus the way to
Jerusalem by stepping on red coats only.

A blanket for the donkey

Color in this blanket, following the guide to colors in the key below.

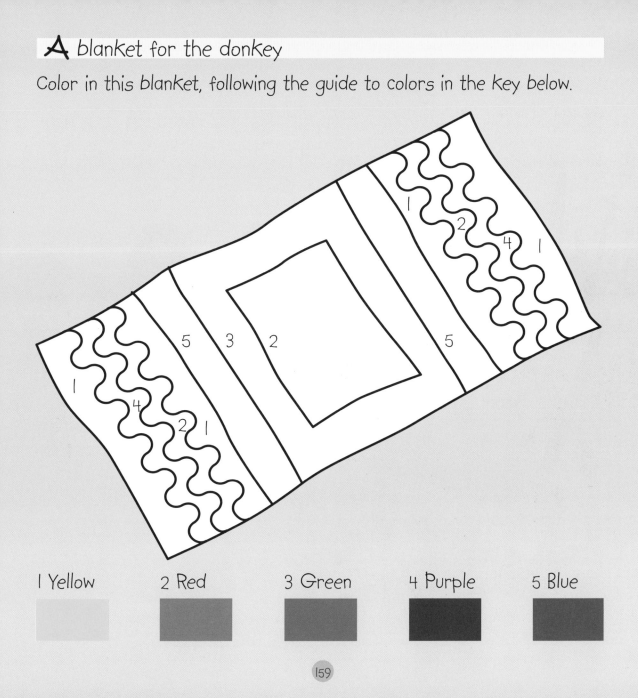

1 Yellow	2 Red	3 Green	4 Purple	5 Blue

Jesus dies on the cross

Jesus had many friends but He also had enemies. They didn't like Jesus. They wanted to get rid of Him. Jesus knew that He was going to die.

So Jesus shared one last special meal with His friends.

That night, He said things to help them remember Him. He wanted the disciples to understand why He had to die. When Jesus died He would put people right with God.

Later that night, Jesus was arrested. But He had done nothing wrong!

Cruel soldiers put a crown of thorns on Jesus' head. His enemies told lies about Him. This was very painful for Him.

Jesus had to carry a heavy cross up a hill. Then He was put on the cross and left to die. Jesus felt very alone.

His mother, Mary, and His friends were very sad.

When Jesus' body was taken down from the cross it was put in a garden tomb. A big stone was rolled across the doorway.

It was a terrible day.

Match the pairs

Draw a line to join each of the helmets that are exactly the same.

Find the crosses

Color in the shapes with a dot. How many crosses can you find?

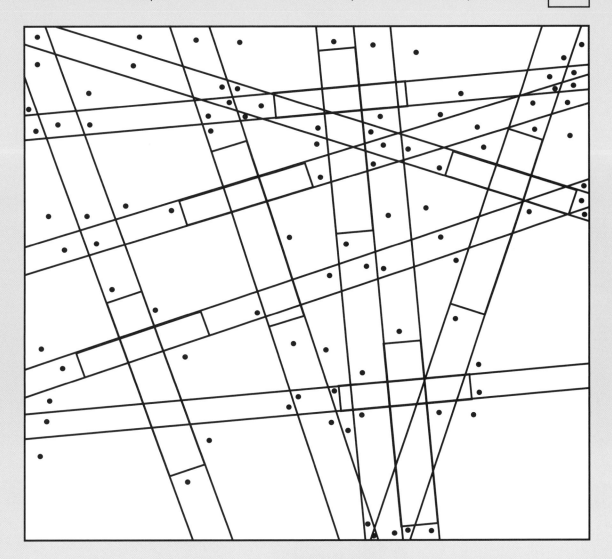

Jesus is risen!

One morning, three days after Jesus had died, three of His friends went to the tomb. The women wanted to put sweet-smelling spices on Jesus' body to honor Him.

When they reached the tomb, they had a big shock. The heavy stone had been rolled away!

The women were afraid. They looked into the tomb. His body was gone! Where was Jesus? Who had taken Him?

Suddenly they saw two men in bright shining clothes standing there.

"Why are you looking for Jesus here?" one man said. "He is not dead, He is alive!"

Full of excitement, the women ran to tell the disciples.

"Jesus is alive!" they said. "The tomb is empty!"

The disciples couldn't believe the news. They didn't understand what the women meant. So, Peter and John ran to the tomb, and sure enough, Jesus was not there!

Mary Magdalene stayed in the garden. It was there that she met and talked with Jesus. He really was alive!

Missing letters

Fill in the missing letters to see what the women told the disciples.

J __ __ __ __ s __ s __ l __ __ __ e!

Big and small

Put a **B** next to the biggest jar and an **S** next to the smallest one.

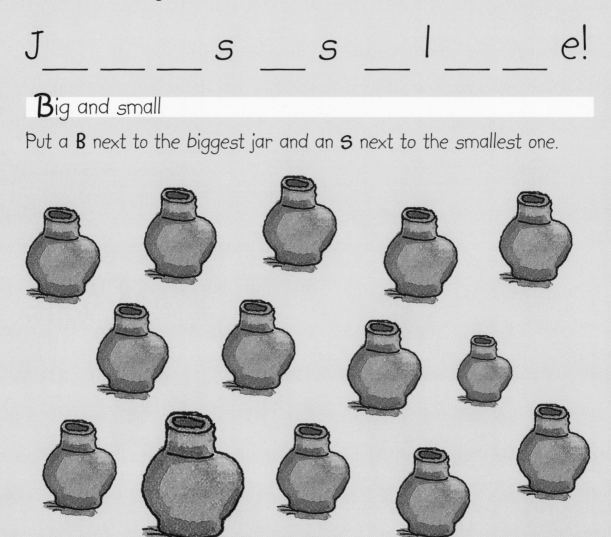

Find and count

Look at the picture below. Count how many of these creatures you can find.

birds ☐   flies ☐   butterflies ☐

Mary Magdalene was so excited! She told her friends that she had seen Jesus, and later they saw Him for themselves. Jesus suddenly appeared to them when they were in a locked room.

The disciples were filled with joy and wonder.

But one disciple, Thomas, was missing. His friends told him the good news, but Thomas did not believe it. He needed to see for himself.

"But we have seen Jesus!" said his friends.

"Well, unless I can see the marks where He was nailed to the cross, I won't believe it," answered Thomas.

A week later, all the disciples were gathered together again. Suddenly Jesus was there in the room with them!

"Look at my hands and feet," He said. "Stop doubting, Thomas!" At last, Thomas believed that Jesus was alive.

Spot the difference

The pictures outside the box all have one detail that is different from the one inside. Mark each difference with a circle.

Complete the picture

Write the number that appears in the blank space next to the correct detail to complete the picture.

Breakfast on the beach

"Let's go fishing," said Simon Peter early one morning. Six friends joined him and they pushed the boat out onto the Sea of Galilee.

They let down their fishing nets into the water and waited... But they did not catch a single fish.

"Throw your nets on the other side of the boat," called a man on the beach. "Then you will catch plenty of fish."

So the fishermen threw their nets on the other side of the boat. When they pulled up the nets, they were full of fish!

"That's Jesus," said one of the fishermen.
Jesus was sitting by a warm fire on the beach.
"Come and eat!" He said.
The disciples were so pleased to see Jesus again.

Count and color

Color in the fish in the net, using a different color for each type.

Count how many different types of fish have been caught. [ ]

How many fish are there in the net? [ ]

Wordsearch

Can you circle all these words from the story in the grid?

b	o	a	t	w	b
i	s	s	m	r	e
r	t	w	s	e	a
d	p	d	q	c	c
m	n	f	i	s	h
f	i	r	e	t	x

fish bird sea

fire beach boat

Counting puzzle

How many seagulls do you see in the picture?

175

Jesus goes to heaven

One day Jesus told His friends something very important.

"Stay in Jerusalem," He said, "I will send you a special helper, God's Holy Spirit. Then you will be filled with power and will tell everyone about Me.

'You will want people all over the world to know about Me. You will tell them what I have taught you, and about My death and resurrection.'

Then Jesus was taken up to heaven, hidden in a cloud. Suddenly two men dressed in white stood beside the disciples.

"Why are you looking up at the sky?" they asked. "Jesus will come back again in the same way as you saw Him go," they promised.

Jesus' friends went back to Jerusalem. There was Peter, John, James and Andrew, Philip and

Thomas, Bartholomew and Matthew, James, Simon, and Judas.
Later, they chose Matthias, another follower of Jesus, to join
their group.

Mary, Jesus' mother, and other women who loved Jesus
joined them. They all prayed to God and waited for the Holy
Spirit to come.

Spot the difference

Eight extra items appear in the bottom picture. Can you circle them?

Picture maze

Help the two groups of people find their way to Jerusalem.

The good news of Jesus

Jesus' special friends often prayed together. One day while they were praying, a sound like blowing wind suddenly filled the room. Whoosh! Bright red flames touched everyone there, but

they did not get burned. The friends found they could speak in many different languages.

This was what Jesus had promised – He had sent them His special helper, God's Holy Spirit. They were so happy!

They went out and told the crowds all about Jesus – how He had been put to death but had come alive again! "I bring you good news," the disciples told the people.

People from other countries came to listen. And they wanted to become friends of Jesus too.

Jesus' friends and the new believers were so excited. They wanted to share the good news of Jesus with everyone.

Colors

Draw a line from each block of color to an item of the same color in the picture below.

yellow red blue green orange

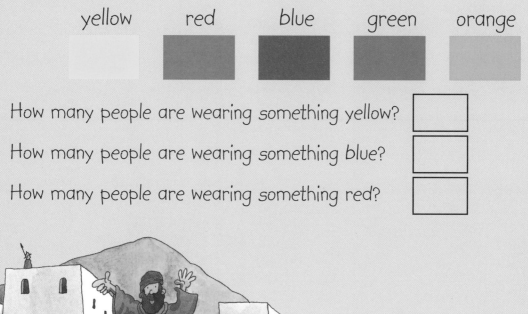

How many people are wearing something yellow?

How many people are wearing something blue?

How many people are wearing something red?

Missing letters

Fill in the missing letters to complete the message the disciples gave to the crowds.

'I b _ _ _ _ g y _ _ _ _ _ d n _ _ _ _ !'

What's wrong?

Can you find eight mistakes in the picture below?
Mark them with a circle.

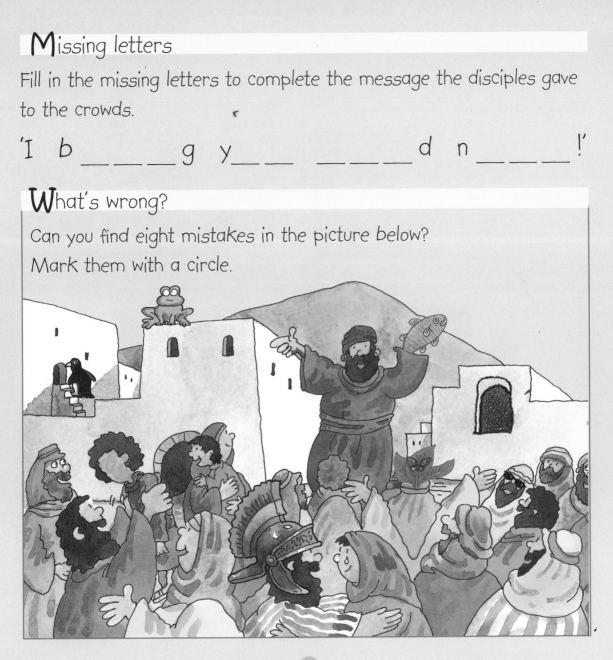

Solutions to the puzzles from the New Testament

Mary's baby Pages 102-103
• There are 8 mice in the picture.

The angel and the shepherds Pages 106-107
• The words are circled on the grid.

• There are 6 sheep.

m	o	d	b	k	p
a	f	r	a	i	d
n	s	k	b	n	s
g	r	t	y	g	s
e	g	o	o	d	a
r	a	n	e	w	s

The wise men worship Jesus Pages 110-111
• The gifts are circled on the picture.

• The correct route is shown on the maze.

The four fishermen Pages 114-115
• a - 2; b - 4; c - 5; d - 3; e - l; f - 6

• b and f are round, a and d are square, c and e are triangles.

• The are 3 red fish, 2 yellow fish, 4 blue fish and 9 fish altogether.

Jesus meets Matthew Pages 118-119
• The wrong things are circled on the picture.

• 1+2 = 3, 2+3 = 5, 1+1 = 2, 3+1 = 4, 2+2 = 4

• There are 8 coins in the bag.

The four good friends Pages 122-123
• Rope 7 is still attached to the stretcher.

• The differences are circled on the picture.

A strong foundation Pages 126-127
• The correct routes are shown on the maze.

• The word pairs are: rock - sand; wise - foolish; long time - quickly; stood firm - fell down

The big storm Pages 130-131

• Only characters a, c, d and e sailed in the boat.

• The opposite of 'storm' is 'calm'.

s	t	o	r	m	v
m	o	c	a	l	m
r	s	w	i	n	d
a	w	a	v	e	s
i	w	a	t	e	r
n	c	k	a	m	s

The girl who Jesus healed Pages 134-135

• There are 6 left hands and 6 right hands.
• The correct heads and bodies are shown below.

The big picnic Pages 138-139

• There are 7 loaves and 7 fishes.

• The odd fish is circled in red.

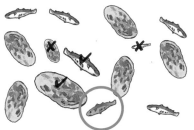

The good neighbor Pages 142-143

• The differences are circled on the pictures.

• A snake and a bird are watching the good neighbor.

The lost sheep Pages 146-147

• There are 6 sheep in the picture. You can see 12 ears and 7 legs.

• The correct path is shown on the maze.

Jesus heals the blind man Pages 150-151

- Character c is not in the picture.
- There are 2 children and 17 grown-ups in the picture.
- The differences are ringed on the picture *below*.

The little tax collector Pages 154-155

- The character is circled on the picture.

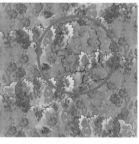

- The odd one out is circled on the picture below.

a lady with a yellow robe	a man with a green headdress	a man in a brown coat	a man with a blue belt

The king rides on a donkey Pages 158-159

- The path is shown on the picture.

Jesus dies on the cross Pages 162-163

- The pairs of helmets are connected below.

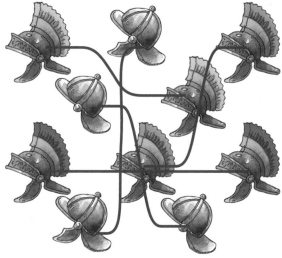

- There are 5 crosses in the drawing.

Jesus is risen! Pages 166-167

• The women said 'Jesus is alive'.

• The smallest and biggest jars are shown in the picture.

• There are 5 birds, 3 flies and 4 butterflies.

Thomas believes Pages 170-171

• The answers are circled on the pictures.

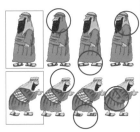

• The correct details are shown here.

Breakfast on the beach Pages 174-175

• 3 different types of fish are in the net. 9 fish have been caught all together.

• The words are circled on the grid below.

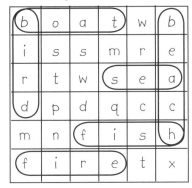

• There are 12 seagulls in the picture.

Jesus goes to heaven Pages 178-179

• The details are circled on the picture.

• The correct routes are shown on the maze.

The good news of Jesus Pages 182-183

• Three people are wearing yellow, seven people are wearing blue, six people are wearing red.

• The message reads 'I bring you good news'

• The mistakes are circled on the picture.

Bible stories can be found as follows:

Old Testament

New Testament

Bible Quiz

Can you answer these quiz questions? There is one question for each story. Look back at the stories if you need help.

1 What are the names of the first people God created? _____

_____

2 Who told Eve to eat the fruit? _____

3 What did Noah build? _____

4 What was the sign of God's promise?

_____

5 Who left his home because God told him to? _____

6 What was the name of Abraham and Sarah's baby? _____

7 How many babies did Rebecca have?

_____

8 Who tricked his father?

_____

9 Who was Jacob's favorite son?

_____

10 What did Joseph's brothers do to him?

_____

11 Who pulled baby Moses from the river?

_____

12 What was the first plague?

_____

13 Which sea did the Israelites cross?

_____

14 Where did the city walls fall down?

_____

15 Who heard God speak in the night?

_____

16 Who was Jesse's youngest son?

_____

17 Who did David fight? _____

18 What brought food to Elijah?

_____

19 What did God send from heaven to light the altar? _____

20 Who washed seven times in the River Jordan? _____

190

21 Who was thrown to the lions?

_____

22 What swallowed Jonah? _____

23 Who gave birth to the baby Jesus?

_____

24 Where was Jesus born?

_____

25 Who followed a star to see Jesus?

_____

26 Which fishermen followed Jesus?

_____

27 What job did Matthew have?

_____

28 Who made a hole in the roof?

_____

29 How many houses were there in Jesus' story? _____

30 Who calmed a storm? _____

31 Whose little girl was brought back to life?

_____

32 What did Jesus use to feed thousands of people? _____

33 Who was a good neighbor?

_____

34 What did the shepherd lose?

_____

35 Why did the beggar need help?

_____

36 What did Zacchaeus do to see Jesus?

_____

37 What did Jesus ride into Jerusalem?

_____

38 Why was the tomb empty?

_____

39 Which disciple doubted that Jesus was alive? _____

40 Who shouted to the fishermen from the shore? _____

41 Where did Jesus go after his resurrection?

_____

42 Who came on the Day of Pentecost?

_____

The answers are on page 192.

Bible Quiz Answers

1 Adam and Eve
2 A snake
3 An ark
4 A rainbow
5 Abraham
6 Isaac
7 Two
8 Jacob
9 Joseph
10 Sold him as a slave
11 An Egyptian princess
12 Nile River turns to blood
13 The Red Sea
14 Jericho
15 Samuel
16 David

17 Goliath
18 Ravens
19 Fire
20 Naaman
21 Daniel
22 A big fish
23 Mary
24 Bethlehem
25 The wise men
26 Simon, Andrew, James and John
27 He was a tax collector
28 Four friends
29 Two houses
30 Jesus
31 Jairus

32 Five loaves and two fish
33 The good Samaritan
34 One sheep
35 He was blind
36 He climbed a tree
37 A donkey
38 Jesus had been raised from the dead
39 Thomas
40 Jesus
41 Heaven
42 The Holy Spirit